Trill Motivation

The Freshest Look at Leadership & Motivation

Books by MrJeffDess

do not hold doors

Haiku from the Home of Reverend Mofo Jones

We Can See Your Privates

Deconstructing Ratchet

2/2/17

The House of Haiku
Presents

Trill Motivation

The freshest look at leadership and motivation

MrJeffDess

grew bap books 2016

DAVID
STAYTRILL

grew bap books

New York City, New York

Copyright © 2016 Jeffrey Dessources

Cover Art by Amjad Khan

www.mrjeffdessworks.com
www.trillornottrill.com
ISBN-13:
978-1530599639

ISBN-10:
1530599636

To Adelani and Adeniran.

My super nephews keep me motivated and inspired every day.

TRILL INTRODUCTION

The word *Trill* has many meanings. Some say it's a mix between True and Real. Some say it's a term that belongs to the city of Houston. *(which is from where I first heard it used)*

Leadership has multiple meanings as well. There are those who say politicians are the epitome of leadership or perhaps great CEO's of business.

Motivation can be defined in a number of ways too. Big speeches or words from an exciting pastor might be the key to motivation.

Trill Motivation is about keeping it fresh and funky at the same time. *Trill Motivation* will push you to transcend and evolve the concepts of leadership.

This type of trill isn't a musical ornament. This type of trill has nothing to do with Young Jeezy. The leadership found in this book isn't your elected official and the motivation you're about to experience isn't about fancy quotes.

Trill Motivation is all about you taking your greatness to the next level. We aren't here to be average.

So as some stay ready.
Over here we'll...

STAY
TRILL
MR

#TrillMotivation 1

TRILL

MOTIVATION

#TrillMotivation 2

GRATITUDE *is the*
type of attitude that will
unlock any door

#TrillMotivation 3

When the baton gets passed to you. Will you grab it and *RUN* with VIGOR?

The great scholar Frantz Fanon once stated, **"Each generation, must out of relative obscurity, discover its mission, fulfill it, or betray it."** The time to fulfill it is right now. The baton from those before you will eventually be passed. If they are unwilling to give it up, you must go grab that baton and go! When it comes to your goals, the finish line is the only option. Allowing others to thwart your efforts isn't an option. When it comes time to achieving greatness, you won't always have time to wait. Let's Get It!

Just because the fat boys broke up doesn't mean you have to stop rockin

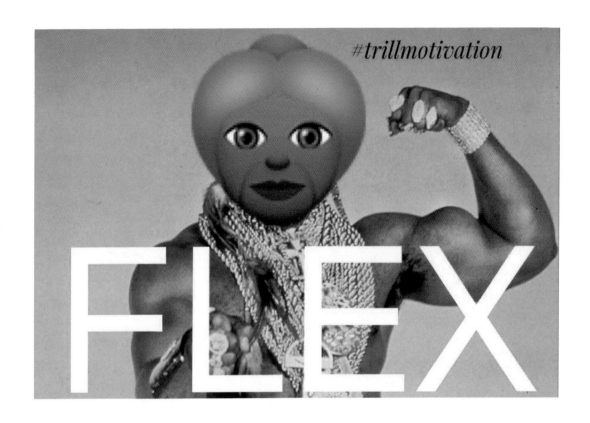

#trillmotivation

FLEX

You are a lot more
powerful than you ever
believed. **Flex on em.**

#TrillMotivation 6

To be at your most CREATIVE you must let go of the fear to fail

Creativity is all about making mistakes. Some of the most brilliant ideas started out as creative mishaps. A few errors never stopped any artist and it won't stop you.

You should respect the game. That should be it. What they eat don't make you shit

What Jay Z eats doesn't make you successful either. Create the lane that works best for you. Letting others dictate the important decisions of your life will ultimately lead to wrong choices. If life were truly a game, there'd be no progress by allowing someone else to take your turn. Stop worrying about what these Sucka MC's are doing. Lastly, there's no need to keep comparing yourself to people who are succeeding differently than you are. Do You!

$$\frac{LOVE \times - HATE \overset{\checkmark}{=} (LOVE)(LOVE)}{LOVE}$$

$$= NO HATE$$

**Eliminate all
the hate from the equation.
Division is dead.**

Dialogue is cute.

Movement is pretty. **ACTION**

is truly **gorgeous.**

Your word is your bond.
Keep it at all times.
Do not deviate from it

#TrillMotivation 11

Treat a new challenge like double dutch. Get loose. Have fun and jump right in

You're going to eventually get hit by the rope, so you might as well go ALL IN. One step towards tackling challenges is to include fun into the equation. Dance like nobody is watching. Jump in without the fear of failure or embarrassment. I'm finna get loose! Let's do it.

Don't ever censor your ability to be unique. Just Stay True.

Photo Credit: Richard Louissant

#TrillMotivation 13

Never sacrifice
Individuality
Common isn't cool

#TrillMotivation 14

FALL IN LOVE WITH WORK

AND EFFORT BEFORE GETTING

MARRIED TO RESULTS

If you're reading this right now. Its not too late to make change in this world.

Drake might have crookedly said it was too late on his album cover, but trust me, there is time. Now, it still may be too late for Meek Mill to effectively retort (I kid, I kid) to the Canadian barrage but not for you. Make the time necessary to impact lives. Often, there's this misconception that great influence must happen in one fell swoop. That is false. Build up your plans to lead and patiently witness the growth. So, don't listen to Drake's message, if your goal is to improve the world, society and yourself. It's never too late. Keep working.

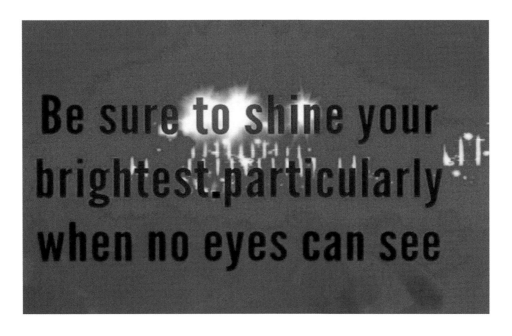

It's not always about how you act when everyone is watching. True leadership will be at its best when no one is around. Recognition is not always required. The same effort presented in front of the masses should be double when they aren't watching. Most of the real work is not always the most visible. Stay Shining!

Struggle will hit much harder than Tyson in his prime. Just stick and move

They will try to find
you whether you *BALL SO HARD*
or you **LEAD SO HARD**

Haters and detractors will find you. Lead so hard that they won't have to search for too long.

The undervalued always have important things to say. Listen up!

No one person is truly iller or more dope than the other. Often times we overlook those considered to be less fortunate simply because of their disposition. The view from what is perceived as "below" provides tremendous insight. It gives us a look at our faults and our ugly sides. Paying attention to those who are usually ignored can lead to enlightening conversations.

Accomplishment is a *DISH* that is best served at all temperatures

Don't worry about preheating. The microwave power settings can be wherever you want them to be. Whether kept at intensely hot or lukewarm, we'll be fine. Accomplishment is something that'll work anywhere at any temperature.

So the Fugees broke up. Doesn't mean we ever have to stop scoring

The Fugees were one of my favorite rap groups of all time. Their second album, The Score, was on steady repeat. When they broke up, I was convinced we'd never hear music like theirs again. What followed were two amazing solo albums. Who knows where the Fugees could have gone... but a break up doesn't stop the show. Everybody falters, but what takes one to the next level is the ability to persevere through the bumpy roads.

OPPORTUNITY DOESN'T ALWAYS KNOCK. AT TIMES IT SNEAKS IN. STAY WOKE.

So many times we get caught in the trap of waiting for opportunities to appear. When they don't, the level of disappointment increases. The best way to avoid missing the boat is to always be ready for the voyage. Look for opportunity underneath every rock and on every path. This mentality keeps you awake and ready. There will come a day when something you never expected will show up to change your life. Having it sneak up, only to go unnoticed is unacceptable. Take charge of every possible opportunity by never underestimating any interaction. Don't miss moments. Keep making them.

There is no gain in RUNNING from a challenge. Time to go toe to toe

Running from a challenge will leave you out of breath and on a path to nowhere. Lace up those kicks and go toe to toe like Evander and Bowe. If you aren't familiar with those two names, look up their fight and watch two pugilists really battle it out. Every challenge is a learning experience, whether you win, lose, or draw. It will make you stronger in the long run and prepare you for future endeavors. Run with wolves instead of letting them chase you.

WE CANNOT LET THE BRASH AND ABRASIVE DICTATE THE CONVERSATION

Very often, the loudest, most brute individuals take over the dialogue. They command attention, not with charisma but with bully tactics or by being louder than others. You must not be drowned out by this brash noise. When it is time to speak up, you have to step up. Leaders can't let the bull in the china shop break all the goods. Take control of the mic.

POPULAR CULTURE
WILL NOT ALWAYS UNDERSTAND
YOUR IDEAS. OH WELL.

Stop **double clicking on distraction.** Stop **swiping away from success.**

Your **MAGIC** will not manifest if you hang with the mediocre

If the people around you aren't driving you to success, then you're on a trip to nowhere. Surround yourself with motivation and the magic will happen. Instead of pulling rabbits out of hats, you'll be pulling solutions out of thin air. You won't be able to hang on to success if you're holding on to failure.

If everyone is
COOL and trendy then no one
is **COOL** and trendy

If you keep feeding your ego you'll one day die of **obesity**

Ego is one of the unhealthiest entities in life. Ego will keep you away from consistently learning from others. It can easily alienate you from other contributing community members. Recognizing your talent is never an issue, but taking it to the next level is the tricky part. A splash of your skills will always be better than drowning people in a pool of trumped up self-esteem. Humility is the anecdote for heavy doses of ego driven decisions.

A TEMPORARY

SETBACK SHOULD NEVER BE A

PERMANENT DEFEAT

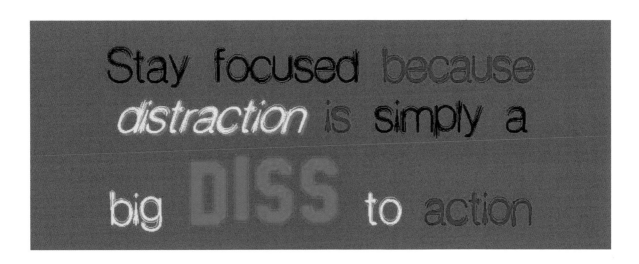

Stop dissing action. Stop it right now. Distraction is a sneaky character and without dedicated focus, said character will do what it takes to knock you off track. Hone in on what truly matters and stick to it.

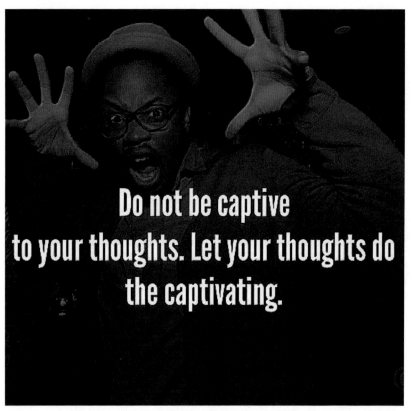

Do not be captive to your thoughts. Let your thoughts do the captivating.

Don't hold back when it comes to change making ideas. Move the masses with invigorating energy and creativity. An audience can be captivated if you're willing to take a chance at being free with your thoughts. We find ourselves being trapped by the fear of taking a chance with our ideas.

Get rid of those shackles now!

The moment you get gassed take a really deep breath and pump all your brakes

Slow down and park yourself next to humility. We are special individuals but always remember, we are special with a lowercased "s." Never get too full of yourself because there'll always be a moments to bring you back to earth. If you can't drive and don't quite get this reference, no worries. Just always remember to slow down baby!

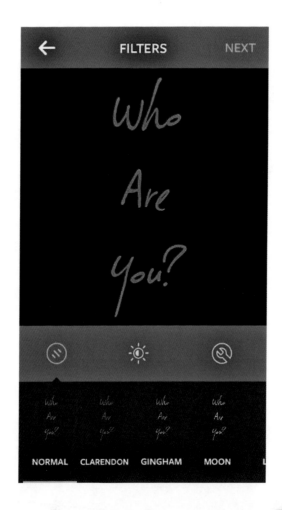

You have to remain
authentic in a world with
so many FILTERS

#TrillMotivation 36

Unpack yourself and travel to a new level of understanding

To truly reach new heights, one must be prepared to deconstruct. Don't leave old baggage hanging around. Look within and discover who you are. To reach the greatest heights, self-investigation is necessary. Unpack and let a new voyage begin.

Minimum wage might not be the best of economic situations, but maximum effort will fill any account. True success doesn't require financial achievement.

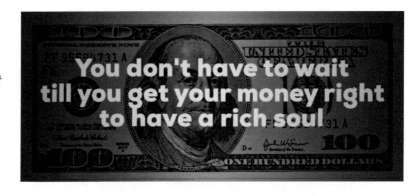

Start by building yourself and you'll build the type of capital necessary for development and leadership. If your mind is right then your money doesn't have to be. Keep your soul rich and you'll always be able to properly cash out.

**Self confidence is
not a fashion trend. It does
not go out of style**

#TrillMotivation 39

Keep an **eye** on the
ones who **stand to benefit**
most from your **stumbles**

Not everyone is looking for you to win. There's no problem in that, but you must keep both eyes open at all times. It is essential to keep those around you, who are willing to stumble with and uplift together. Avoid the company of those who are awaiting you to slip up just so they can slip in. Keep your head on swivel as move towards your greatness.

Sometimes M&M'S don't melt at all. Always have alternative plans.

Things will not always go as planned. The best way to be prepared is to have a plan A, B, and C in your back pocket. If it's supposed to melt in your mouth but today decided to melt in your hand, you better be ready. Getting rattled by unscheduled moments shouldn't shake you.

Chillin out. Maxin. Relaxin all cool is not enough. Need that work

TRILL MOTI VAT ION

If you are always seeking attention you won't find any treasures

Do not be afraid
to challenge the darkness or
the unknown ahead

When you challenge the unknown, the results will be excellent. When you know what's coming ahead of time, there won't be any growth or change. To win and to lead is to embrace the unpredictable.

Never stop doing
your best because someone is
not showing you love

When arrogance clings to you. Don't be afraid to Harlem Shake it off.

#TrillMotivation 46

You cannot truly savor victory until you've tasted defeat

Embrace the moments of struggle. Do so with the mindset that potential losses are ALL learning lessons. Your wins are beautiful, but to know that they came from the work you put in makes them even more exceptional. Be prepared to taste defeat; it'll only be a precursor to bigger and better things. The way to achieve this, takes confidence in the work that you're putting in. If your goals are easy to attain, you need some new ones. Victory is that much greater when you can remember all the lessons you had to learn to make it to the top.

IMAGINATION
is a tool that can be used to fix anything

Imagination is one of the only things that knows no limits. Any problem can be solved if you dig deep to the place where imagination lives. Immerse yourself in the unknown. Your creative sense is more powerful than you think. If there's something you've never thought of before, keep thinking. If there's something you've never tried to do before, go get it done. Understanding the power of imagination will give you the power to change the world.

Excellence is your presence. Never tense. Never hesitant. **Be Big**

Be Big.

Be so hungry that when life deals you some lemons you could just eat them

I wish someone would try and feed me lemons. Hunger is the type of drive that will help you achieve seemingly unattainable goals. Don't be afraid to crave the highest levels of success. Hungry, Hungry Hippos was a wild children's game I grew up playing. Players would just bang away at the game looking to feed plastic toy Hippos as many marbles as possible. At the end of all the chaos, the hungriest hippo came out victorious. I know this was about lemons but damn that game was fun and filled with teachable moments. Never stop fighting and eating up every challenge you are faced with. Trust me when I say, that overcoming adversity always tastes better than the simple solutions.

If you're starting from
the bottom there's no reason
you can't flip the script

If you're starting from
the bottom there's no reason
you can't flip the script

#TrillMotivation 51

FLY

If you wanna
you got to give up the things
that will weigh you
down

IF THEY AREN'T SERVING

TRUTH AT YOUR TABLE THEN IT'S

TIME TO EAT ELSEWHERE

#TrillMotivation 53

Moral victories
are for minor league coaches
Think big. Be major.

Moral victories are not a bad thing. They are great representations of effort taking place. The minor leagues are also a wonderful accomplishment. Around these trill parts though, we strive to reach even higher levels of excellence. Don't listen to anyone who says you can't reach that height. Think above such a mindset. Championships aren't the only victories but they are pretty damn impressive and totally attainable. Start being Major right now. Be the most Major thinking person in your office. When you walk into class put in the work ethic so that everyone including the professor recognizes how Major you are. Be a Major artist. Be a Major professional. Be a Major student leader. Think Major and travel with Major thinkers and watch the victories of life start piling up.

Attempting to keep an eagle in a shoebox is impossible

You have the wings and ability to soar. Don't get boxed in by limitations; especially limitations created by others. When you have the talent and passion, there is no holding back. Trust your ability to fly through clouds and not be deterred by restrictions. Think bigger and outside of any box ever created.

Make commitments to love and compassion and you'll connect to the world

PASSION
LOVE
THE MOMENTS
STAY TRILL.

#TrillMotivation 56

Good things might come to
those who wait. Great things come to
those who go get it

Some of the darkest events in life were made to brighten up your way

As children, they would put night lights in our rooms to give us a glimpse of light. The darkness shouldn't be feared. It's a place that will heighten your senses. Dark moments in life seem scary at first. They are painful while happening. All of these sentiments will eventually provide clearer paths towards success. Trusting the darkness will get you to the light every time.

Procrastination is a trophy for losers.
Winners get it done.

WE ARE WINNERS

#TrillMotivation 59

**If people try to
come at your neck simply start
Loosening the tie**

Adversity is coming your way whether you like it or not. When it arrives, invite that bad boy inside and show them what you got. Look challenge right in the eye and don't flinch. When you're prepared and confident in your ability, there's not a thing you won't be able to handle. Oh, and if you don't wear ties...scarves, chokers, and ascots are applicable

Your comfort zone should be a location filled with risks and challenges

The comfort zone as designed is never going to be a place of empowerment. Redesign your space and turn it into somewhere that's consistently challenging you to do better. Get comfortable in a room filled with risk and watch the difference. Results will begin to appear in the face of adversity. I challenge you to go someplace out of your comfort zone. DO IT RIGHT NOW!

The weekend is not just off days and high vocals.
Every moment counts

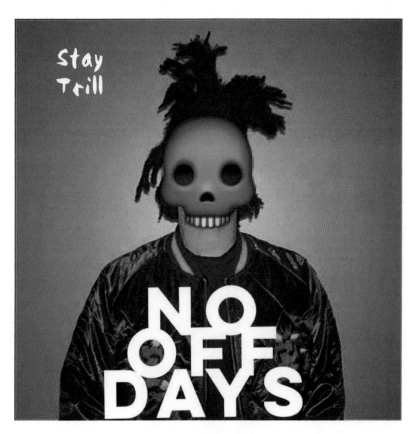

#TrillMotivation 62

Deconstruct culture
Deconstruct relationships
Deconstruct yourself

Although traditionally used in a literary or philosophical sense, deconstruction plays a role in a quest to reach below the surface. To dig, is to self-deconstruct. The point is not to destroy but to actually breakdown, build up and restructure positive trains of thought. Doing this will help you recognize that many of your thoughts are unnatural and constructed. These same thoughts are created and dependent on extrinsic values. Expansion of self can only happen with deconstruction. Time to DIG within.

the world is yours if
you're willing to take control
at the toughest times

One minute of some movement is greater than an hour of intention

:24

ALARM   AM   PM

Time waits for no one. A minute of movement will always get you further than intention, alone. Do us all a favor. Get up and go! Forward progress won't exist on simply thought processing. Make firm decisions and make them happen. Time will only tell, but trust, it'll speak volumes if you put your foot down and move.

The most dangerous
BEAST in the zoo is still trapped.
Go find your freedom

You will never be invited to freedom. Crash the party and dance

When it comes to *life*
Sometimes it's a marathon.
Sometimes it's *a sprint.*

Versatility will get you everywhere. Keep those extra pair of sneakers nearby, because one never knows when it'll be time to run or switch up the race. In either case preparation is key. Make sure you aren't frantically trying to catch up, when some groundwork and research would have given you a comfortable lead. One of my favorites rap bars is, **"Sometimes I rhyme slow. Sometimes I rhyme quick".** *Always be ready to adapt and handle the situation.*

Be an instrument
that is instrumental in
making others move

#TrillMotivation 69

Old Dirty Bastard didn't jump on a stage and interrupt the 1997 Grammy awards for you to be out here basking in your throwback Thursday ideas. If you aren't pushing yourself towards creating new ideas then everyone loses. When a creative roadblock appears, embrace your youthful side. Traveling there leads to embracing innocence and unclouded innovation. Old Dirty would be proud of you.

You will never be Beyoncé but remember she'll never be you

The greatest thing about yourself is that nobody else can be you. We each possess a unique quality which separates us from the rest of the world. If that trait has yet to be discovered, no worries. Dig deeper and locate the beauty within that no one else can have. Take your thoughts to a place they've never traveled before. Beyonce might be able to dance better than me (still debatable), but I bet my haiku skills are superior. Now, that might have been a bit comical but even such a comparison isn't essential to one's growth or development. Work hard and be the master of your own domain. You have the gifts to be the greatest but they will never be found or opened if there's a concern about being like others.

DETERMINATION

needs to be a part of your diet everyday

EAT YUM

DeteR MINATION

Press pause on posing.
Click cancel on those costumes
Forget being fake

Embrace authenticity. To do so, requires transparency. Be honest with who you are and people will listen a lot more carefully. Don't hide your true self for the sake of appearing or looking a certain way. Costumes may be cool on Halloween, but it's rather silly to rock that sexy nurse outfit all year round. Take a genuine approach to life. Cut out all the posing and press play on legitimacy.

In most cases you're running away from yourself and not real danger

Always be cognizant of your audience. Be consistent with messages of empowerment because you truly never know how many people are listening. Your range of influence likely reaches further than you'd ever expect. They will respond, so be careful with what you're communicating.

Just in case Miley Cyrus is *still* twerking you should *still* be working

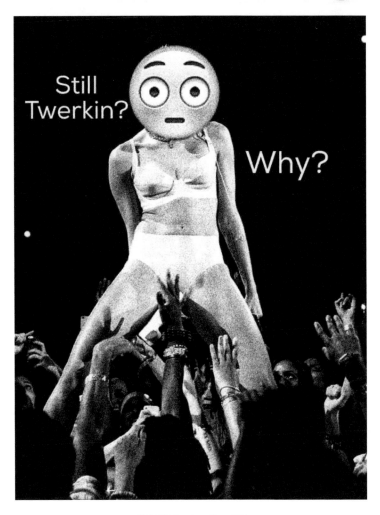

FLASHING

You don't have to smile for each photograph just be prepared for the flash.

#TrillMotivation 78

Inconvenience can be insightful. Discomfort can drive decisions

Embrace the difficult times in your life. They will ultimately serve as a key to a room filled with development and excellence. Don't ever write off tough situations and trepidation as automatic defeats. Use them to catapult yourself to the top.

**Go to the lion's
den and get comfortable.
Now learn how to ROAR**

*The more you interact with adversity, the better you'll be at handling it.
Walk into the lion's den and grab yourself a seat. Get comfortable in
spaces you aren't used to or were once afraid of. Take a chance and
instead of getting bitten, you'll find yourself speaking the language of
kings.*

Positive outlooks
are your passports to any
place you're scared to go

That time mama said
knock em out she was talkin
about all your fears

When mama tells you to knock out the fears, you do what mama says. You can truly overcome anything you're afraid of by taking it right to that challenge. Fear doesn't stand a chance of going a full 12 rounds with you.

In the presence of asthmatic acrobats you've gotta breathe easy

Not everyone is going to be able to handle difficult times. When a test presents itself, fully expect some people to overreact or lose their cool. It will be up to you to take a deep breath and remain calm as a leader. Be the voice of reason when the chatter is too loud. If others aren't willing to do it, and they are hyperventilating then step and breathe easy.

Do not look to the people who want to see your failure. **Look past them**

#TrillMotivation 84

MICHAEL JORDAN missed more shots than he made but what do you remember?

Bumps in the road are inevitable but when you continue to strive for and achieve excellence those losses become an afterthought. Make people remember your moments of glory by raising the bar and taking your greatness to the next level. Don't dwell on the missed opportunities. Continually create new chances and keep scoring. As you soar towards your goals be sure to fly like no one has ever done so before.

When it's all said and done *investing* in yourself will always PAY OFF//

A diverse point of
view is an optimum way
to stay sharp in life

IF YOU'RE NOT READY TO BE WRONG AT TIMES, YOU WILL NEVER GET IT RIGHT.

Newsflash! You will not always be right. Recognize this and you'll avoid being a Sucka MC. Humility is a great strength that can only be achieved if you're ready to be wrong.

If you're not prepared to check yourself then you will likely wreck yourself

#TrillMotivation 89

> ## Don't let *yesterday* dictate your moves of today and of tomorrow

The greatest parts of yesterday won't always mean tomorrow will be excellent. In addition, the negative aspects of your past won't determine how your future will be. Never get too high and never get too low. Stay as consistent as possible. Stick to the plan and you'll be dominant on any day of the week.

Any marriage to *mediocrity* needs to end in a divorce

Say **NO**
To
Mediocrity

#TrillMotivation 91

Have the **gumption** to hustle with vultures and not turn into dinner

Commitment has no expiration date. There's no running out of that.

You'll never have to give it a second smell because, commitment never spoils. You'll never have a bowl of cereal and not enough commitment because commitment never runs out. You never have to check the stamp and the date because commitment has never heard of an expiration date. For all of that to happen though, you have to put in the work. Commitment will always be there for you but will return the favor. Doing so will lead to great results.

#TrillMotivation 93

Tasting defeat should always make you hungry for the next victory

Sucka MCs don't see success and are fine if you're blind right with them

If you're a person striving for the best, ideally everyone around you would be too. Unfortunately the world doesn't work like that. You'll be met with detractors for any number of reasons. Those folks could be haters filled with jealousy or even your friends with stagnant mentalities. Your vision to see these hurdles and run up, over and through them if necessary is a key to success. Sucka MCs are fine with the status quo. They're more than ok with stepping over you to reach mundane levels. You are not that type of person. Avoid the distraction created by these people. Leave them behind and if they aren't willing to be pushed towards winning, then pull yourself away.

Just because you can't find the remote doesn't mean you can't CHANGE channels

The tools necessary for change won't always be lying around. Not being able to find them, doesn't mean forward progress has to be halted. Trust me, I've misplaced that remote control before, but you better believe, I won't be held hostage. Get up and change the channel. Stand up and turn on the movement.

Putting another person down will never bring you to a new height

If you deserve an pie do not let them give you just the slice

Settling is for SuckaMCs. If you are striving for excellence then the results should match the expectations. Settling is about choices; choosing subpar options won't help in achieving goals. A partial life is what you'll be living if you don't fight for what you deserve. The only person that can keep you from getting that entire pie is yourself. Don't leave your greatness in the hands of the mediocre.

Don't ever censor your ability to be unique. Keep it TRILL

#TrillMotivation 99

> **Haters never take sick days. Put in the work and make great moves daily**

We've got to stop letting these hecklers speak for us and get wins on our watch. Negativity shows up diligently, hard hat on ready to work. We've got to combat that with our own positive efforts. The only way to do so is by making great moves every day. Don't just be good. Be Great! Save those sick days for someone else.

#TrillMotivation 101

STAY
TRILL

MR

#TrillMotivation 102

ACKNOWLEDGEMENTS

I would like to first thank my editors, Benjamin Ciesinski and Ruth Nineke. They guided this text to the right space. The mistakes are my own and has nothing to do with their excellence

Thanks to my fellow educators and speakers, whose continue to motivate Jullien Goron, James Robilotta, Scott Siegel, Alexandros Orphanides, Rahiel Testfamariam, Lenny Williams and Antonio Talamo; you've all been amazing colleagues and friends.

Shouts to my brothers in the "group chat." Your daily doses of weeniqueness and brilliance pushes me closer towards my goals.

In 2015, a group of student leaders were committed to greatness. They turned into the 1st class of the Sword and Shield Leadership Society. Never has a group of students inspired me so much.

To my sister Dr. Nancy Adegoke and my parents Jacques and Andrele Dessources for always being present, even when I'm sometimes absent.

Immense thanks to all the young people who I've spoken to, to all my former RA's, to all the students I've advised and to all the future generations I will continue to reach out to.

May we all stay Trill, TOGETHER.

You are always welcome back to the House of Haiku.

ABOUT THE AUTHOR

MrJeffDess is a writer, public speaker, emcee, professor and student affairs professional. He currently serves as the editor in chief of *TrillorNotTrill.com* which is a blog that infuses culturally relevant content with the world of education, student development and leadership.

Book MrJeffDess

Bring MrJeffDess to your campus, company, conference or event!

Keynotes
Workshops
Emcee an Event
Leadership Training
Performances

For a complimentary consultation to decide if MrJeffDess is the right speaker for you, contact him at
MrJeffDess@gmail.com or www.mrjeffdessworks.com

Made in the USA
Charleston, SC
11 November 2016